~A BINGO BOOK~

Connecticut
Bingo Book

COMPLETE BINGO GAME IN A BOOK

QUI TRANSTULIT SUSTINET

Written By Rebecca Stark
Educational Books 'n' Bingo

ISBN 978-0-87386-500-5

Educational Books 'n' Bingo

Printed in the U.S.A.

DIRECTIONS

INCLUDED:

List of Terms

Templates for Additional Terms and Clues

2 Clues per Term

30 Unique Bingo Cards

Markers

1. **Either cut apart the book or make copies of ALL the sheets. You might want to make an extra copy of the clue sheets to use for introduction and review. Keep the sheets in an envelope for easy reuse.**

2. Cut apart the call cards with terms and clues.

3. Pass out one bingo card per student. There are enough for a class of 30.

4. Pass out markers. You may cut apart the markers included in this book or use any other small items of your choice.

5. Decide whether or not you will require the entire card to be filled. Requiring the entire card to be filled provides a better review. However, if you have a short time to fill, you may prefer to have them do the just the border or some other format. Tell the class before you begin what is required.

6. There are 50 terms. Read the list before you begin. If there are any terms that have not been covered in class, you may want to read to the students the term and clues before you begin.

7. There is a blank space in the middle of each card. You can instruct the students to use it as a free space or you can write in answers to cover terms not included. Of course, in this case you would create your own clues. (Templates provided.)

8. Shuffle the cards and place them in a pile. Two or three clues are provided for each term. If you plan to play the game with the same group more than once, you might want to choose a different clue for each game. If not, you may choose to use more than one clue.

9. Be sure to keep the cards you have used for the present game in a separate pile. When a student calls, "Bingo," he or she will have to verify that the correct answers are on his or her card AND that the markers were placed in response to the proper questions. Pull out the cards that are on the student's card keeping them in the order they were used in the game. Read each clue as it was given and ask the student to identify the correct answer from his or her card.

10. If the student has the correct answers on the card AND has shown that they were marked in response to the *correct questions,* then that student is the winner and the game is over. If the student does not have the correct answers on the card OR he or she marked the answers in response to *the wrong questions,* then the game continues until there is a proper winner.

11. If you want to play again, reshuffle the cards and begin again.

Have fun!

TERMS INCLUDED

Algonquian	Thomas Hooker
Ethan Allen	Immigrant(s)
American Robin	King Philip
Benedict Arnold	Legislative Branch
Border(s)	Long Island Sound
Bridgeport	Judicial Branch
Charter Oak	Motto
Coastal Lowlands	Mountain Laurel
Samuel Colt	Mystic Seaport
Connecticut Compromise	New Haven
Connecticut River	New Netherland
Connecticut Valley Lowland	Nickname
County (-ies)	Oyster
Prudence Crandall	Pequot
Dominion of New England	Praying Mantis
Dutch	Royal Charter
Eastern New England Upland	Sperm Whale
Executive Branch	Harriet Beecher Stowe
Flag	Taconic Section
Fundamental Orders	Uncas
Garnet	Union
Geographic Regions	War of 1812
Nathan Hale	Noah Webster
Hartford	Western New England Upland
Hartford Convention	Yale University

Barbara M. Peller

Additional Terms

Choose as many additional terms as you would like and write them in the
squares. Repeat each as desired.
Cut out the squares and randomly distribute them to the class.
Instruct the students to place their square on the center space of their card.

Barbara M. Peller

Clues for
Additional Terms

Write three clues for each of your additional terms.

<table>
<tr>
<td>

_____

1.

2.

3.

</td>
<td>

_____

1.

2.

3.

</td>
</tr>
<tr>
<td>

_____

1.

2.

3.

</td>
<td>

_____

1.

2.

3.

</td>
</tr>
<tr>
<td>

_____

1.

2.

3.

</td>
<td>

_____

1.

2.

3.

</td>
</tr>
</table>

Barbara M. Peller

Algonquian

1. The name "Connecticut" is an ___ word that means "long river."
2. ___-speaking tribes in the area that is now Connecticut included Mahicans, Mohegans, Pequots, and others.

Ethan Allen

1. This Revolutionary War Patriot was born in Litchfield. He was the leader of the citizens' militia known as the Green Mountain Boys.
2. ___ and Benedict Arnold were instrumental in the capture of Fort Ticonderoga, which gave colonists their first victory over British troops in the War for Independence.

American Robin

1. The ___ is the state bird.
2. The___ is a type of thrush.

Benedict Arnold

1. This general originally fought for the American Continental Army but defected to the British Army. He was born in Norwich, Connecticut, in 1741.
2. His name has become synonymous with the word "traitor."

Border(s)

1. Massachusetts, Rhode Island, and New York ___ Connecticut.
2. The Atlantic Ocean ___ Connecticut to the south.

Bridgeport

1. ___ is the most populous city in the state.
2. The Beardsley Zoo is located in ___.

Charter Oak

1. The ___ Incident refers to the hiding of Connecticut's royal charter that had been granted by King Charles II.
2. The Connecticut ___ was on Samuel Wylly's property.

Coastal Lowlands

1. The Connecticut ___ form a narrow strip of land, 6 to 16 miles wide; it runs along the southern shore of the state at Long Island Sound.
2. Lower than most of Connecticut, this region is characterized by low ridges and beaches and   harbors along the coast.

Samuel Colt

1. This inventor and industrialist was born in Hartford, Connecticut.
2. His invention made the mass-production of the revolver possible.

Connecticut Compromise

1. The ___ was an agreement that large and small states reached during the Constitutional Convention of 1787.
2. The ___ kept the bicameral legislature proposed by Madison, which called for proportional representation in the lower house and equal representation in the upper house.

Connecticut Bingo

Barbara M. Peller

Connecticut River 1. The Native American word *"Quinnehtukqut,"* which means "beside the long tidal river," was first used to refer to this river. 2. The ___ was discovered by Dutch explorer Adriaen Block.	**Connecticut Valley Lowland** 1. The ___ is a long, narrow land area that extends from northern Massachusetts to southern Connecticut. It was created by the Connecticut River. 2. The state is divided into two sections, often called the eastern highland and the western highland; they are separated by the ___.
County (-ies) 1. There are 8 ___ in Connecticut. 2. It is not surprising that Fairfield ___ is the most populous in the state. It includes four of the state's largest cities: Bridgeport, Stamford, Norwalk and Danbury.	**Prudence Crandall** 1. ___ is the official state heroine. She established the first school in New England for African-American women in 1833. She and her students faced prejudice and violence, and the school was forced to close after 18 months. 2. Her school is now is a National Historic Landmark. It is located in Canterbury.
Dominion of New England 1. In 1686 King James II created the ___, which comprised Massachusetts, Vermont, New Hampshire, Connecticut, and Rhode Island and later New York and East and West Jersey. 2. Sir Edmund Andros was governor of the ___ during most of its three-year existence.	**Dutch** 1. The first European settlers in the Connecticut area were the ___. 2. In 1614 Adriaen Block, a ___ explorer, sailed along the Connecticut coast and up the Connecticut River.
Eastern New England Upland 1. The Connecticut section of the ___ stretches from Connecticut to Maine and is heavily forested. 2. Most of eastern Connecticut is in the ___ geographic region; it is characterized by narrow river valleys and low hills.	**Executive Branch** 1. The governor is head of the ___. The present-day head of the ___ is [fill in]. 2. The governor, lieutenant governor, secretary of the state, treasurer, comptroller and attorney general are all part of the ___ of government.
Flag 1. The background of the state ___ is azure blue. In the center is a white shield with three grapevines, each with three bunches of purple grapes. 2. Like the Great Seal, the state ___ includes a ribbon with the state motto on it: *"Qui transtulit sustinet."* Connecticut Bingo	**Fundamental Orders** 1. The document known as the ___ of Connecticut was the basic law of Connecticut Colony from 1639 to 1662. Thomas Hooker, John Haynes, and Roger Ludlow were influential in framing the document. 2. The ___was one of the earliest constitutions in America. It is the reason for the state nickname, Constitution State. **Barbara M. Peller**

Garnet
1. Almandine ___ is the state mineral.
2. Connecticut is one of the finest sources in the world of almandine ___, which is a deep violet-red.

Geographic Regions
1. Even though it is a small state, Connecticut can be divided into 5 distinct ___.
2. The geographic regions are the Taconic Section; the Western New England Upland, or Highland; the Connecticut Valley Lowland; the Eastern New England Upland, or Highland; and the Coastal Lowlands.

Nathan Hale
1. ___ is the official Connecticut state hero. He was born in Coventry, Connecticut, in 1755.
2. This Patriot is known for his last words before being hanged: "I only regret that I have but one life to give for my country."

Hartford
1. ___ is the capital of the state and the third largest city in the state.
2. ___ is sometimes called Insurance City because of all the insurance companies that are headquartered here.

Hartford Convention
1. The ___ was a secret meeting of Federalist delegates from Connecticut, Rhode Island, Massachusetts, New Hampshire, and Vermont. It met during the War of 1812.
2. The ___ opposed the War of 1812 and the policies of President Madison. This secret meeting was unpopular and was a factor in the collapse of the Federalist Party.

Thomas Hooker
1. ___ and John Haynes founded the Colony of Connecticut as a haven for Puritans in 1636.
2. ___ is often called the Father of Connecticut. He was influential in framing the Fundamental Orders.

Immigrant(s)
1. Factories in Bridgeport, New Haven, Waterbury and Hartford attracted many European ___ to Connecticut in the early part of the 20th century.
2. Almost 30% of the state's population was made up of ___ by 1910.

King Philip
1. ___'s real name was Metacomet. He was the chief of the Wampanoag Indians.
2. ___'s War was a conflict between Native Americans and English colonists and their Native American allies in 1675–78.

Legislative Branch
1. The ___ of state government is called the General Assembly. It comprises the House of Representatives and the Senate.
2. The ___ of government writes new laws and changes laws that exist.

Long Island Sound
1. The Connecticut River runs through the center of the state and empties into ___.
2. ___ is Connecticut's outlet to the Atlantic Ocean.

Connecticut Bingo

Barbara M. Peller

Judicial Branch	**Motto**
1. The Supreme Court is the highest court of the ___ of government. It is made up of a chief justice and six associate justices. 2. The ___ is made up of the Supreme Court, the Appellate Court, the Superior Court, and the Probate Court.	1. The state ___ is *"Qui Transtulit Sustinet."* It means, "He Who Transplanted Still Sustains." 2. The state ___ is on a ribbon on both the Great Seal and the state flag.
Mountain Laurel	**Mystic Seaport**
1. The ___ is the official state flower. 2. The ___ has fragrant, star-shaped, white and pink flowers.	1. The re-creation of the freedom schooner *Amistad,* the official state tall ship, was constructed at ___ . 2. ___ is known for its collection of sailing ships and boats and for the re-creation of a 19th-century seafaring village.
New Haven	**New Netherland**
1. ___ is the second largest city in the state. Only Bridgeport is larger. 2. Yale University is located in ___ .	1. The Dutch West India Company offered an incentive to settlers of ___ . It was called the patroonship system. 2. According to the Dutch West India Company, settlers of ___ were considered to be servants of the company.
Nickname	**Oyster**
1. Connecticut's ___ is The Constitution State. 2. Connecticut got its nickname because of the Fundamental Orders.	1. The state shellfish is the Eastern ___ . 2. The Eastern ___ thrives in Connecticut's tidal rivers and coastal estuaries. The state has a thriving ___ industry.
Pequot	**Praying Mantis**
1. The 1638 Treaty of Hartford settled the ___ War, but the ___ were not a part of it. Their lands went to the towns along the Connecticut River. 2. In the ___ War the colonists were allied with the Mohegan and Narragansett.	1. The ___ is the state insect. 2. This insect gets its name from its habit of standing motionless on its four hind legs, with its two forelegs raised as if in meditation.
Connecticut Bingo	**Barbara M. Peller**

Royal Charter	**Sperm Whale**
1. King Charles II granted the Colony of Connecticut a ___. 2. King James II tried to revoke the ___ that had been granted to the Colony of Connecticut by his brother, King Charles II.	1. This marine mammal is the state animal. 2. Now on the endangered list, the ___ was at one time important to the state's economy. New London was the most significant whaling port in the 19th century.
Harriet Beecher Stowe	**Taconic Section**
1. This author was born in Litchfield, Connecticut, in 1811. 2. She is best known as the author of *Uncle Tom's Cabin.*	1. The ___ is in the northwestern corner of the state. Mount Frissell, the highest point in the state at 2,380 feet, is in this area. 2. The ___ goes from the Housatonic River to the New York border and extends north into Massachusetts.
Uncas	**Union**
1. This renowned warrior allied his forces with the English colonists in the Pequot War. 2. ___ was a sachem of the Mohegan; his alliance with the English colonists made the Mohegan the leading regional Indian tribe in lower Connecticut.	1. Connecticut manufacturers played a major role in supplying the ___ Army and Navy with weapons, ammunition, and military materiel during the Civil War. 2. Connecticut was one or the original 13 states. It became the 5th state to join the ___ on January 9, 1788.
War of 1812	**Noah Webster**
1. Essex was attacked by Great Britain on April 8, 1814, during the ___. 2. The Battle of Stonington took place during the ___ . A substantial British naval squadron unsuccessfully attacked this small coastal village.	1. He was the author of the first truly American dictionary. He was born in West Hartford on October 16, 1758. 2. His first dictionary, *A Compendious Dictionary of the English Language,* appeared in 1806. In 1828 he published his *American Dictionary of the English Language.*
Western New England Upland	**Yale University**
1. The highest areas of Connecticut are in the ___; however, the highest point in the state is not in this region. 2. The ___ is characterized by steep hills, ridges and rivers. This geographic region runs into parts of Massachusetts and Vermont.	1. ___ is a private Ivy League research university located in New Haven. 2. ___ is the third-oldest institution of higher education in the U.S.

Connecticut Bingo

Barbara M. Peller

Connecticut Bingo

Oyster	Algonquian	American Robin	Flag	Border(s)
Eastern New England Upland	Ethan Allen	Noah Webster	Long Island Sound	Royal Charter
War of 1812	Legislative Branch		New Haven	Western New England Upland
Union	Praying Mantis	Uncas	King Philip	Motto
Mystic Seaport	Geographic Regions	Prudence Crandall	Harriet Beecher Stowe	Hartford Convention

Barbara M. Peller

Connecticut Bingo

Union	War of 1812	Hartford	Pequot	Immigrant(s)
Motto	Dominion of New England	Coastal Lowlands	Praying Mantis	Mountain Laurel
Connecticut Compromise	Geographic Regions		Nathan Hale	Uncas
New Netherland	Nickname	Legislative Branch	Yale University	Border(s)
Royal Charter	Noah Webster	Prudence Crandall	Eastern New England Upland	Harriet Beecher Stowe

Barbara M. Peller

Connecticut Bingo

Geographic Regions	Uncas	Dominion of New England	King Philip	War of 1812
Motto	Ethan Allen	Samuel Colt	Algonquian	Garnet
Praying Mantis	Noah Webster		Mountain Laurel	Benedict Arnold
Legislative Branch	Connecticut Compromise	Mystic Seaport	New Netherland	Hartford
Harriet Beecher Stowe	Connecticut River	Prudence Crandall	Yale University	Immigrant(s)

Barbara M. Peller

Connecticut Bingo

Legislative Branch	Mountain Laurel	American Robin	Connecticut River	Immigrant(s)
Judicial Branch	Charter Oak	Algonquian	Pequot	War of 1812
New Haven	New Netherland		Hartford Convention	Flag
Uncas	Ethan Allen	Noah Webster	Prudence Crandall	Coastal Lowlands
Connecticut Valley Lowland	Royal Charter	Bridgeport	Harriet Beecher Stowe	Western New England Upland

Connecticut Bingo: Card No. 4

Barbara M. Peller

Connecticut Bingo

Royal Charter	Border(s)	Praying Mantis	Coastal Lowlands	Connecticut River
Judicial Branch	Uncas	Samuel Colt	Nathan Hale	Ethan Allen
American Robin	Western New England Upland		Long Island Sound	Fundamental Orders
Hartford Convention	Immigrant(s)	Oyster	Yale University	County (-ies)
Dominion of New England	Prudence Crandall	War of 1812	Legislative Branch	New Haven

Connecticut Bingo: Card No. 5

Barbara M. Peller

Connecticut Bingo

Benedict Arnold	Mountain Laurel	Hartford	Immigrant(s)	Western New England Upland
King Philip	Praying Mantis	County (-ies)	Algonquian	War of 1812
Pequot	Connecticut Valley Lowland		Charter Oak	Nathan Hale
Prudence Crandall	Mystic Seaport	Yale University	Bridgeport	American Robin
Motto	Coastal Lowlands	Oyster	New Haven	Dutch

Barbara M. Peller

Connecticut Bingo

Oyster	Mountain Laurel	Fundamental Orders	Uncas	Dominion of New England
Motto	Immigrant(s)	Geographic Regions	Ethan Allen	Judicial Branch
Western New England Upland	Flag		Nathan Hale	Charter Oak
Legislative Branch	New Netherland	Samuel Colt	Union	Connecticut Compromise
Prudence Crandall	Connecticut River	Yale University	Bridgeport	Benedict Arnold

Connecticut Bingo: Card No. 7

Barbara M. Peller

Connecticut Bingo

New Haven	Mountain Laurel	Executive Branch	King Philip	Charter Oak
Judicial Branch	American Robin	Pequot	Western New England Upland	Coastal Lowlands
Dutch	Connecticut River		Immigrant(s)	Border(s)
Harriet Beecher Stowe	Legislative Branch	Union	Connecticut Valley Lowland	New Netherland
Noah Webster	Prudence Crandall	Bridgeport	Praying Mantis	Motto

Barbara M. Peller

Connecticut Bingo

Nathan Hale	Dominion of New England	Geographic Regions	Dutch	Connecticut River
Connecticut Valley Lowland	Immigrant(s)	New Haven	Praying Mantis	Mountain Laurel
Garnet	Oyster		Ethan Allen	Executive Branch
County (-ies)	Border(s)	Mystic Seaport	Long Island Sound	Fundamental Orders
New Netherland	Yale University	Samuel Colt	Union	Hartford Convention

Barbara M. Peller

Connecticut Bingo

Union	King Philip	Charter Oak	Pequot	Dutch
Western New England Upland	Coastal Lowlands	Algonquian	Ethan Allen	Immigrant(s)
Connecticut River	Mountain Laurel		Flag	Connecticut Compromise
Mystic Seaport	Hartford Convention	County (-ies)	Yale University	Garnet
Samuel Colt	Motto	Hartford	Royal Charter	New Haven

Barbara M. Peller

Connecticut Bingo

Benedict Arnold	Mountain Laurel	Praying Mantis	County (-ies)	Motto
Executive Branch	Garnet	Long Island Sound	Nathan Hale	Algonquian
Judicial Branch	Immigrant(s)		Hartford	Geographic Regions
Samuel Colt	War of 1812	Yale University	Connecticut River	Union
Connecticut Valley Lowland	Prudence Crandall	Oyster	Bridgeport	Dominion of New England

Connecticut Bingo: Card No. 11

Barbara M. Peller

Connecticut Bingo

Dominion of New England	Border(s)	Garnet	King Philip	Nathan Hale
Geographic Regions	Motto	American Robin	Bridgeport	Ethan Allen
Oyster	Fundamental Orders		Western New England Upland	Pequot
Prudence Crandall	New Netherland	Immigrant(s)	Union	Judicial Branch
Mountain Laurel	Executive Branch	Connecticut River	Connecticut Valley Lowland	Coastal Lowlands

Barbara M. Peller

Connecticut Bingo

County (-ies)	Border(s)	Benedict Arnold	Garnet	Western New England Upland
American Robin	Executive Branch	Immigrant(s)	Nathan Hale	Connecticut Compromise
King Philip	Coastal Lowlands		Geographic Regions	Fundamental Orders
New Haven	Yale University	Charter Oak	Connecticut River	Union
Prudence Crandall	Hartford Convention	Bridgeport	Oyster	Long Island Sound

Barbara M. Peller

Connecticut Bingo

Eastern New England Upland	Immigrant(s)	Praying Mantis	Nathan Hale	Connecticut Valley Lowland
Coastal Lowlands	Oyster	Garnet	Ethan Allen	Mountain Laurel
County (-ies)	Flag		Hartford	Samuel Colt
Hartford Convention	Yale University	Connecticut River	Charter Oak	Benedict Arnold
Prudence Crandall	Pequot	Connecticut Compromise	Motto	New Haven

Barbara M. Peller

Connecticut Bingo

Long Island Sound	Nathan Hale	Praying Mantis	Dominion of New England	King Philip
Benedict Arnold	Hartford	Algonquian	American Robin	Connecticut Valley Lowland
Western New England Upland	Oyster		War of 1812	Mountain Laurel
Prudence Crandall	Garnet	Executive Branch	Yale University	County (-ies)
Motto	New Netherland	Bridgeport	Dutch	Geographic Regions

Barbara M. Peller

Connecticut Bingo

Charter Oak	Garnet	Executive Branch	Dutch	Nickname
Pequot	Connecticut Compromise	Fundamental Orders	Judicial Branch	Flag
County (-ies)	Border(s)		Western New England Upland	Geographic Regions
Legislative Branch	Coastal Lowlands	Prudence Crandall	Long Island Sound	Union
Connecticut Valley Lowland	Taconic Section	Bridgeport	New Netherland	Mountain Laurel

Barbara M. Peller

Connecticut Bingo

Samuel Colt	Sperm Whale	Thomas Hooker	Garnet	Eastern New England Upland
Long Island Sound	Connecticut Valley Lowland	Yale University	Flag	Fundamental Orders
Nathan Hale	New Haven		Taconic Section	Executive Branch
Hartford Convention	Motto	Union	Praying MantisMantis	Connecticut Compromise
Mystic Seaport	County (-ies)	Dominion of New England	King Philip	Border(s)

Connecticut Bingo: Card No. 17

Barbara M. Peller

Connecticut Bingo

Dutch	Connecticut River	Coastal Lowlands	County (-ies)	Pequot
Mountain Laurel	Samuel Colt	Mystic Seaport	Western New England Upland	Connecticut Valley Lowland
Nathan Hale	Connecticut Compromise		Thomas Hooker	American Robin
Border(s)	Algonquian	Yale University	Union	Hartford
Taconic Section	Garnet	Praying Mantis	Sperm Whale	Benedict Arnold

Connecticut Bingo: Card No. 18

Barbara M. Peller

Connecticut Bingo

Western New England Upland	Benedict Arnold	Garnet	Executive Branch	Union
Long Island Sound	King Philip	Mountain Laurel	Dominion of New England	Flag
Sperm Whale	Connecticut River		Ethan Allen	War of 1812
Hartford	Taconic Section	Mystic Seaport	New Netherland	Thomas Hooker
American Robin	Nickname	Motto	New Haven	Bridgeport

Barbara M. Peller

Connecticut Bingo

Eastern New England Upland	Sperm Whale	King Philip	Garnet	Bridgeport
Coastal Lowlands	Geographic Regions	Judicial Branch	Mystic Seaport	Pequot
Border(s)	Fundamental Orders		Legislative Branch	Algonquian
Royal Charter	Noah Webster	Harriet Beecher Stowe	New Netherland	Taconic Section
Uncas	New Haven	Nickname	Union	Thomas Hooker

Connecticut Bingo: Card No. 20

Barbara M. Peller

Connecticut Bingo

Long Island Sound	Benedict Arnold	Judicial Branch	Garnet	Royal Charter
Border(s)	Thomas Hooker	Charter Oak	Executive Branch	Oyster
Connecticut Compromise	Motto		Sperm Whale	Praying Mantis
Mystic Seaport	Dominion of New England	Taconic Section	Hartford Convention	New Haven
Legislative Branch	Nickname	Bridgeport	Samuel Colt	New Netherland

Barbara M. Peller

Connecticut Bingo

Dutch	Hartford	Thomas Hooker	American Robin	County (-ies)
Pequot	King Philip	War of 1812	Executive Branch	Ethan Allen
Coastal Lowlands	Flag		Oyster	Fundamental Orders
Taconic Section	Hartford Convention	New Netherland	Algonquian	Judicial Branch
Nickname	Samuel Colt	Sperm Whale	Connecticut Compromise	Legislative Branch

Barbara M. Peller

Connecticut Bingo

Charter Oak	Sperm Whale	Dominion of New England	American Robin	Bridgeport
Benedict Arnold	Eastern New England Upland	Motto	Long Island Sound	Algonquian
Hartford	County (-ies)		Harriet Beecher Stowe	Oyster
Connecticut Compromise	Nickname	Taconic Section	Samuel Colt	New Netherland
Royal Charter	Noah Webster	New Haven	Mystic Seaport	Thomas Hooker

Barbara M. Peller

Connecticut Bingo

Charter Oak	New Haven	Eastern New England Upland	Sperm Whale	Executive Branch
Thomas Hooker	Bridgeport	Judicial Branch	Pequot	Oyster
Fundamental Orders	Dutch		County (-ies)	Connecticut Compromise
Royal Charter	Harriet Beecher Stowe	Taconic Section	Samuel Colt	Border(s)
Uncas	Legislative Branch	Nickname	King Philip	Noah Webster

Connecticut Bingo: Card No. 24

Barbara M. Peller

Connecticut Bingo

Legislative Branch	Judicial Branch	Sperm Whale	Praying Mantis	Thomas Hooker
Algonquian	Border(s)	Long Island Sound	Charter Oak	Ethan Allen
Hartford Convention	Executive Branch		Harriet Beecher Stowe	Taconic Section
War of 1812	Royal Charter	Noah Webster	Nickname	Flag
Bridgeport	Eastern New England Upland	Coastal Lowlands	Connecticut Valley Lowland	Uncas

Barbara M. Peller

Connecticut Bingo

Thomas Hooker	Sperm Whale	Hartford	Pequot	Dutch
Mystic Seaport	King Philip	Executive Branch	Eastern New England Upland	Charter Oak
Hartford Convention	Harriet Beecher Stowe		Flag	Legislative Branch
Samuel Colt	American Robin	Royal Charter	Nickname	Taconic Section
Fundamental Orders	Connecticut Valley Lowland	Praying Mantis	Noah Webster	Uncas

Barbara M. Peller

Connecticut Bingo

Hartford	Coastal Lowlands	Sperm Whale	Eastern New England Upland	Geographic Regions
Royal Charter	Harriet Beecher Stowe	Long Island Sound	Taconic Section	Ethan Allen
Yale University	Noah Webster		Nickname	Legislative Branch
Dutch	Benedict Arnold	Judicial Branch	Uncas	Algonquian
Connecticut Valley Lowland	Flag	Thomas Hooker	War of 1812	Fundamental Orders

Connecticut Bingo: Card No. 27

Barbara M. Peller

Connecticut Bingo

Hartford	Eastern New England Upland	War of 1812	Sperm Whale	Charter Oak
Geographic Regions	Thomas Hooker	Harriet Beecher Stowe	Pequot	Flag
Noah Webster	Connecticut Compromise		Fundamental Orders	Mystic Seaport
Union	Dutch	Motto	Nickname	Taconic Section
American Robin	Nathan Hale	Connecticut Valley Lowland	Uncas	Royal Charter

Barbara M. Peller

Connecticut Bingo

Thomas Hooker	Eastern New England Upland	Dutch	Long Island Sound	Nathan Hale
New Netherland	Mystic Seaport	Judicial Branch	Fundamental Orders	War of 1812
Hartford Convention	Harriet Beecher Stowe		Ethan Allen	Sperm Whale
Geographic Regions	Royal Charter	Immigrant(s)	Nickname	Taconic Section
Charter Oak	Executive Branch	Uncas	Benedict Arnold	Noah Webster

Barbara M. Peller

Connecticut Bingo

Connecticut River	Sperm Whale	Pequot	Nathan Hale	Taconic Section
Algonquian	Eastern New England Upland	Hartford	Flag	Ethan Allen
Hartford Convention	County (-ies)		Fundamental Orders	Judicial Branch
Uncas	Benedict Arnold	American Robin	Nickname	Harriet Beecher Stowe
Royal Charter	Western New England Upland	Noah Webster	Thomas Hooker	War of 1812

Connecticut Bingo: Card No. 30

Barbara M. Peller